# ERIN PATTERSON

The True Story of the

Mushroom Murders and

Australia's Most Bizarre Triple

Homicide

Ella Elizabeth Smith

## Disclaimer

This book is based on real events. While every effort has been made to ensure accuracy, some details have been reconstructed from court documents. The author makes no claims as to the guilt or innocence of any individual beyond what has been legally determined.

This work is intended for informational and educational purposes only and is not meant to glorify or exploit tragedy.

# Table of Contents

**Introduction**     **10**

**Chapter One**     **12**

Erin Patterson — A Life in the Background     12

Married Simon Patterson, Later Divorced     14

Maintained Contact with In-Laws Despite

Separation     16

Known to Be Quiet, Private, and Somewhat

Withdrawn     18

No Criminal Record Before the Incident     20

**Chapter Two**     **22**

The Patterson Family — Victims and Survivors     22

Heather Wilkinson: Gail's Sister     25

Ian Wilkinson: Local Pastor, Heather's Husband     27

All Were Respected Members of Their

Community     30

Invited to Lunch as a Gesture of Reconciliation     32

**Chapter Three**     **34**

The Lunch That Changed Everything     34

Guests Reported the Meal Tasting "Normal"          36

All Four Became Gravely Ill by the Next Day          38

Erin Did Not Eat the Same Portion—Or Claimed

Not To          40

Initial Speculation Suggested Food Poisoning,

Later Revealed to Be Death Cap Mushrooms          43

**Chapter Four**          **46**

A Town in Shock          46

Community Members Express Disbelief and Fear 48

Speculation Grows Over Whether It Was

Accidental or Deliberate          51

Erin Gives Initial Interviews Denying Wrongdoing  54

**Chapter Five**          **57**

Death Cap Mushrooms — A Killer Ingredient          57

Symptoms: Delayed Onset, Organ Failure,

Especially the Liver and Kidneys          60

Easily Mistaken for Edible Mushrooms          63

Fatal if Not Treated Early          65

Uncommon in Domestic Food Poisonings, More

So in Deliberate Cases          67

**Chapter Six**                                          **69**

    Erin's Shifting Story                            69

    Later Added That She Also Used Dried

    Mushrooms from Her Pantry                       71

    Stated She Never Intended to Harm Anyone        73

    Claimed to Have Been Hospitalized with

    Symptoms Herself                                75

    Contradictions Noted by Police and Media        77

**Chapter Seven**                                        **80**

    The Dehydrator and the Deleted Files            80

    Police Allege It Was Used to Prepare the

    Mushrooms                                       82

    Erin's Phone Was Factory Reset                  84

    Several Digital Files Deleted, Raising Questions

    About Intent                                    86

    Investigators Retrieved Internet Search History

    and Deleted Texts                               88

**Chapter Eight**                                        **90**

    A Pattern of Deceit                             90

    Erin's Ex-Husband, Simon Patterson, Had a

    History of Unexplained Illness                  93

Simon Was Invited to the Lunch But Did Not

Attend                                          96

Police Viewed Her Behavior as Strategic and

Misleading                                      99

**Chapter Nine**                               **102**

Arrest and Charges                             102

Bail Was Denied Initially                      107

Case Formally Enters Pre-Trial Proceedings     109

**Chapter Ten**                                **111**

The Mushroom Murders Trial Begins              111

Prosecution Argued Erin Acted Knowingly and

Deliberately                                   113

Defense Claimed It Was a Tragic Accident       116

Case Drew International Media Attention         119

**Chapter Eleven**                             **122**

Eight Days on the Stand                        122

Maintained: She Never Intended Harm            124

Struggled Under Prosecutorial

Cross-Examination                              126

Her Demeanor and Tone Became Part of Public

Debate                                         128

**Chapter Twelve**      **131**

Survivor on the Stand — Ian Wilkinson      131

Underwent a Liver Transplant      133

Described Shock and Grief Over Losing His

Wife      135

His Survival Allowed Prosecutors to Reconstruct

the Timeline      137

**Chapter Thirteen**      **140**

The Verdict      140

Erin Patterson Found Guilty on All Charges      142

Public Reaction Was Intense—Many Expressed

Relief, Others Shock      144

Media Outlets Dubbed It One of Australia's

Most Bizarre Homicides      146

**Chapter Fourteen**      **148**

Sentencing and the Road Ahead      148

Erin Faces Life Imprisonment      150

Families of the Victims Seek Closure and

Justice      152

Appeals Process Remains Open but Uncertain      154

Case Raises Broader Questions About

Culpability and Domestic Trust                    156

**Epilogue**                                      **159**

# Introduction

It was meant to be a simple lunch—a gesture of goodwill between a woman and her former in-laws. The table was set in a quiet home in rural Victoria. Beef Wellington was on the menu. Four guests sat down. Three would never leave the hospital.

What unfolded in the days that followed left Australia stunned. The culprit wasn't a masked stranger or an armed intruder. It was a familiar face: Erin Patterson, a quiet, unassuming mother who claimed it was all a terrible accident. Yet the evidence told another story—one of poison hidden in plain sight, and a family gathering turned fatal.

As investigators peeled back the layers, a darker narrative emerged—one of fractured relationships, fatal ingredients, and a host who insisted on her innocence. The question that haunted the nation wasn't just how it happened, but why.

And in the quiet that followed, that question still lingers.

# Chapter One

## Erin Patterson — A Life in the Background

Erin Patterson's story begins in the quiet surroundings of rural Victoria, a region known more for farmland and family ties than for scandal. Her early years unfolded in a small-town environment, where community life was subdued and daily routines followed familiar patterns. There is little public information about her childhood, but those who encountered her over the years recalled a girl who didn't attract attention. She appeared to be a product of her environment—unassuming, soft-spoken, and rooted in a lifestyle that values privacy over spectacle.

She grew up far from the pressures of metropolitan life, and this small-town upbringing significantly shaped her adult identity. Erin was not known for ambition or public engagement. Instead, her personality seemed to align more with the quiet rhythms of country life—introverted, modest, and mostly unnoticed. These early experiences set the tone for how she would later conduct herself: away from the spotlight, even in times of intense scrutiny.

# Married Simon Patterson, Later Divorced

In adulthood, Erin married Simon Patterson, a man whose family was well-regarded in the same Victorian region. Their marriage appeared ordinary to outsiders, with no outward signs of dysfunction or hostility. Together, they had two children and established a home in the local area. The Patterson family was known to be involved in the community and carried a reputation for decency and civility.

At some point, however, the marriage began to unravel. The reasons for their separation remain private, but by the time of the fatal lunch in 2023, Erin and Simon were no longer living together. Their relationship, though legally dissolved, continued to be complicated. Despite the breakdown of their marriage, they lived relatively close to each other and continued to raise their children while navigating post-divorce dynamics.

Simon himself would later become a silent figure of intrigue in the unfolding investigation. His absence from the lunch, despite allegedly being invited, raised questions. But before the tragedy, their split had seemed uneventful to most observers—two people who had gone their separate ways without public acrimony.

# Maintained Contact with In-Laws Despite Separation

One of the most striking aspects of Erin's post-divorce life was her continued relationship with her ex-husband's parents, Don and Gail Patterson. Even after her marriage to Simon ended, Erin remained connected to the Patterson family. It was a connection that appeared civil, if not particularly close, and it played a pivotal role in what was to come.

Maintaining ties with former in-laws after a divorce is not uncommon, especially when children are involved. In Erin's case, the contact seemed to signal an effort—at least on the surface—to keep peace within the broader family circle. She invited them to her home for meals, spoke to them regularly, and still played a role in family matters. It was this lingering connection that led to the ill-fated lunch on July 29, 2023.

That ongoing relationship would later become central to the investigation. Why would Erin serve a meal to people she no longer had a strong familial obligation to? Was this an act of kindness, or did it mask something more sinister? The fact that Don and Gail accepted the invitation suggested a level of trust that had survived the marital breakdown—trust that would soon prove fatal.

# Known to Be Quiet, Private, and Somewhat Withdrawn

People who had encountered Erin over the years described her in similar terms: reserved, quiet, and distant. She did not participate actively in community functions, and she rarely socialized beyond her immediate circle. Neighbors said she often kept to herself, offering polite greetings but rarely engaging in deeper conversation.

She wasn't known for hobbies or causes, nor did she cultivate a social media presence that might offer insight into her thoughts or values. Erin's interactions were typically limited to school-related activities for her children or simple errands in town. There were no outbursts, no rumors, and no drama—at least not until 2023.

This withdrawn personality made it difficult for investigators and journalists alike to paint a clear portrait of who she was. In some ways, her silence became a kind of shield. As the Mushroom Murders case gained public attention, Erin's reticent nature added to the mystery. Was she simply overwhelmed by grief and confusion—or was she hiding behind a lifetime of emotional detachment?

# No Criminal Record Before the Incident

Before the deaths of Don, Gail, and Heather, Erin Patterson had never been in trouble with the law. There was no criminal record attached to her name, no history of violence, fraud, or reckless behavior. Her past, at least in legal terms, was clean.

This absence of a criminal background made the events surrounding the fatal lunch all the more bewildering. How could a woman with no history of malice or misconduct suddenly be implicated in a case involving lethal mushrooms and a trail of dead relatives? It was a question that perplexed the public and investigators alike.

Her spotless record didn't eliminate suspicion, but it complicated the narrative. Erin Patterson was not a known danger. There were no warning signs that something like this could happen. No neighbors had called the police, no friends had reported erratic behavior. On paper, she had lived an ordinary, law-abiding life—until three people were dead and a fourth barely clinging to life.

# Chapter Two

## The Patterson Family — Victims and Survivors

Don and Gail Patterson were no strangers to the community of Korumburra in Victoria's South Gippsland region. Elderly but active, they were respected and well-liked in the tight-knit town where family names still carried weight. Don had retired after a long career, while Gail, equally dedicated to family and community, remained involved in local events. They were the parents of Simon Patterson, Erin's ex-husband, and had once welcomed her into their family with open arms.

Despite Simon and Erin's eventual divorce, Don and Gail had remained in intermittent contact with Erin, primarily because of their grandchildren. Maintaining family unity for the sake of the children seemed to be a priority for them. There were no public indications of conflict or hostility between the former in-laws, and on the surface, the family dynamic remained cordial. So, when they were invited to Erin's home for lunch on July 29, 2023, they accepted—perhaps as part of a broader gesture of healing after the strain of the separation.

The decision to attend that lunch would prove fatal. Both Don and Gail became gravely ill within 24 hours of consuming the Beef Wellington Erin served, which later was believed to contain death cap mushrooms. Their health declined rapidly. Despite hospital efforts, neither survived. Their deaths were a profound loss not only to their family but to a community that had long held them in high regard.

# Heather Wilkinson: Gail's Sister

Heather Wilkinson, the third person to die after attending the infamous lunch, was more than just a guest. She was Gail Patterson's sister, and by all accounts, she shared her sister's calm demeanor, warm personality, and strong sense of family. Heather had spent much of her life in the same general region of Victoria, close enough to remain closely connected to both Gail and the extended Patterson family.

She was known for her gentleness and reliability, the kind of person who showed up when it mattered and remained a steady presence in family life. Heather had a reputation for being kind-hearted and community-minded. When she received the lunch invitation from Erin, there appeared to be no hesitation. She came with her husband Ian, expecting a pleasant afternoon in familiar company.

Heather's sudden illness after the meal mirrored that of Don and Gail—severe gastrointestinal distress followed by liver failure. Despite swift medical intervention, her condition was irreversible. She died in the days following the lunch, becoming the third fatality and deepening the mystery surrounding what had gone so wrong.

Her death sent shockwaves not only through the family but also through the broader network of churchgoers and friends who had come to know her as a nurturing, spiritual woman. Her passing, coupled with that of her sister, turned the tragedy into a family catastrophe.

# Ian Wilkinson: Local Pastor, Heather's Husband

Ian Wilkinson was, in many ways, the most publicly known of the four lunch guests. A local pastor in the Korumburra area, Ian had spent decades ministering to the spiritual needs of his congregation. He was seen as a moral compass, a source of comfort and guidance to those facing hardship. His sermons were well-attended, and his reputation as a kind and measured man was widespread.

Ian attended the lunch with his wife Heather and, like the others, fell ill soon afterward. His condition became critical within days, and he was placed on life support as doctors fought to keep his organs from shutting down. Unlike the other three, however, Ian survived—barely. He underwent an emergency liver transplant that ultimately saved his life, though the recovery process was long, painful, and emotionally devastating.

His survival brought mixed emotions: relief that at least one guest had pulled through, but also sorrow for the profound loss of his wife and close friends. For Ian, the tragedy was both personal and public. He not only lost his wife but was pulled into a national investigation that scrutinized every detail of that deadly afternoon.

In the months that followed, Ian would remain largely silent, refraining from public comment as detectives built their case. His voice, when it did emerge through legal channels or church updates, was one of grief but also forgiveness—a rare trait in the wake of such devastating loss.

# All Were Respected Members of Their Community

What made the deaths all the more shocking was who the victims were. These were not strangers. They were pillars of the community, people known for their kindness, dependability, and integrity. In small-town Victoria, everyone knows someone, and these individuals have long, visible histories in the region.

Don and Gail Patterson were longtime residents who had raised a family and contributed quietly to local life. Heather Wilkinson was known for her warmth and supportiveness. Ian Wilkinson was not just respected but revered—a spiritual leader whose words carried weight in times of joy and crisis.

Their reputations made the tragedy deeply personal to many in Korumburra and surrounding areas. It was not simply the story of three people who died after a meal. It was the loss of trust in a close community, the unsettling realization that something so dark could happen in such familiar surroundings.

# Invited to Lunch as a Gesture of Reconciliation

The lunch invitation was extended by Erin Patterson under the guise of a reconciliation effort. Reports indicated that Erin had framed the gathering as an opportunity to rebuild bridges, particularly with Don and Gail, following the strain caused by her divorce from Simon. It was meant to show goodwill—a family gesture, simple and sincere.

The presence of Heather and Ian further reinforced the idea that this was not a confrontational setting but rather a peaceful one. Erin reportedly told friends and police that the meal was prepared with love and shared with everyone, including herself. She later claimed that she too fell ill after eating the same dish, though her symptoms were less severe.

That offer of reconciliation, if genuine, has since been overshadowed by doubt. Investigators, media outlets, and the public began to question everything about the gathering—why it was scheduled, how the food was prepared, and whether it was ever truly meant to bring peace. Whether the lunch was a tragic accident or a carefully plotted act remains at the heart of a legal and moral debate that continues to unfold.

# Chapter Three

## The Lunch That Changed Everything

On July 29, 2023, Erin Patterson prepared what was supposed to be a heartfelt family lunch in her home in Leongatha, a quiet town in regional Victoria. The centerpiece of the meal was Beef Wellington, a traditional English dish consisting of beef tenderloin coated with pâté and duxelles, wrapped in puff pastry, and baked. It's a recipe known for being complex and time-consuming—hardly a casual choice for a family meal, which made it all the more curious.

Erin later told investigators that she had gone to great effort to make the dish from scratch, including the preparation of the mushroom duxelles—a finely chopped mixture of mushrooms, onions, and herbs sautéed in butter. According to her version of events, the meal was meant as a peace offering, a way to rebuild strained ties with her former in-laws and extended family.

Although the gesture appeared gracious, it would come to be viewed through a far darker lens. The preparation of a mushroom-based meal, especially one involving finely minced fungi, would take on horrific significance in the days to come.

# Guests Reported the Meal Tasting "Normal"

None of the guests—Don and Gail Patterson, Heather Wilkinson, or Ian Wilkinson—suspected anything unusual as they ate the lunch. By all accounts, the meal was consumed without complaint. No one reportedly commented on a strange taste, texture, or smell. Erin herself claimed that nothing about the Beef Wellington stood out as odd or inedible.

In interviews that surfaced later, sources close to the victims confirmed that the dish had been enjoyed at the time. No one stopped eating halfway through or pushed their plate away in suspicion. For the guests, it was just a home-cooked lunch—a friendly gathering between family members who were trying to reconnect after years of emotional distance.

This detail became a crucial part of the investigation. If the food had tasted off, it might have raised an immediate alarm. Instead, the "normal" taste gave the dish an air of innocence, allowing any dangerous ingredients to pass unnoticed. It also raised questions about how the mushrooms—later identified as among the most toxic in the world—were able to be incorporated without detection.

# All Four Became Gravely Ill by the Next Day

By the following day, all four guests had fallen critically ill. Symptoms began with violent nausea, vomiting, and diarrhea—textbook indicators of severe food poisoning. At first, family members believed it might be a common case of gastroenteritis or salmonella, but the rapid deterioration of the victims' health quickly ruled out those possibilities.

The illness unfolded in two phases, as is common with ingestion of death cap mushrooms. First came the gastrointestinal storm—an onslaught of abdominal pain, cramping, and dehydration. This was followed by a brief window in which some victims appeared to stabilize, creating false hope. But behind the scenes, the real damage had begun: the liver and kidneys were under assault, steadily shutting down as the toxins ravaged their systems.

Heather Wilkinson, Don Patterson, and Gail Patterson died within days of the meal. Ian Wilkinson, the only one to survive, required an emergency liver transplant and remained in critical condition for weeks. His survival would later prove instrumental to the investigation.

The fact that four healthy adults could go from enjoying a meal together to fighting for their lives within 24 hours stunned the community and alarmed health authorities. The question on everyone's mind was the same: What had they eaten—and why?

# Erin Did Not Eat the Same Portion—Or Claimed Not To

One of the most scrutinized aspects of the case was Erin Patterson's claim that she did not eat the same portion of Beef Wellington as her guests. In her statement to police, Erin said she had prepared the dish for the family but had eaten only part of it—possibly a different serving altogether. She explained that she had leftovers stored in the refrigerator and later consumed them without becoming seriously ill.

At one point, she also told authorities she had taken the remaining food to the hospital where Ian was being treated, reportedly to show doctors what the group had eaten. However, this act raised further suspicions, particularly after she allegedly threw out a food dehydrator around the same time, an item which some believed might have been used in the preparation of the mushrooms.

Her relatively mild symptoms stood in stark contrast to the fate of her four guests. Though she admitted to experiencing some illness, it was nowhere near the level of severity that her visitors endured. Critics were quick to ask why. Had she truly consumed the same food? Was her illness exaggerated or even fabricated? Or, more darkly, had she known to avoid the contaminated portion?

These inconsistencies became central to the police investigation, and Erin's shifting explanations were closely dissected by both detectives and the media. What began as a tragic family lunch was rapidly evolving into a potential homicide case.

# Initial Speculation Suggested Food Poisoning, Later Revealed to Be Death Cap Mushrooms

At first, the public and media believed the tragedy to be a case of food poisoning. Even seasoned medical professionals initially leaned toward common foodborne illnesses as the cause, particularly because of how quickly symptoms had developed. But when the bloodwork and toxicology reports came back, they told a much more chilling story.

Authorities revealed that the victims had not succumbed to ordinary foodborne bacteria but rather had ingested Amanita phalloides, commonly known as death cap mushrooms. These mushrooms are among the most poisonous on Earth. Just one cap is enough to kill an adult, and there is no known antidote. The toxins they release, primarily amatoxins, destroy liver cells and disrupt the body's protein synthesis, leading to organ failure.

The mushrooms are difficult to distinguish from edible varieties to the untrained eye. Death caps often grow in the wild around Victoria, especially near oak trees. This raised a critical question: Did Erin unknowingly use wild mushrooms she had foraged, or did she deliberately include them, aware of the consequences?

As this information became public, the narrative shifted from one of misfortune to one of possible premeditation. Investigators began treating the case not as a tragic mistake but as a potential triple homicide.

# Chapter Four

## A Town in Shock

Within days of the tragic deaths of Don and Gail Patterson and Heather Wilkinson, the media descended on the small town of Leongatha. The story had all the elements of a national sensation: a quiet rural community, respected victims, and an unnerving twist involving one of the world's deadliest mushrooms. Newspapers across Victoria and Australia quickly picked up the story, and soon, headlines like "Lunch Turns Deadly in Leongatha" and "Mushroom Murders Rock Victoria" dominated the news cycle.

The term "Mushroom Murders" was coined almost instantly—short, gripping, and eerily descriptive. News outlets ranging from local papers to major broadcasters like ABC and The Age covered the incident with growing intensity, often featuring images of Erin Patterson walking quietly past photographers, her face hidden beneath a wide-brimmed hat or hoodie. With each passing day, public interest grew. The fact that such a seemingly ordinary lunch had led to three deaths and a near-fatality kept the nation transfixed.

The phrase "Mushroom Murders" stuck. It became the shorthand for a complex, unfolding investigation, and a source of deep anxiety for the communities involved. Leongatha, once a town barely noticed beyond regional borders, now found itself at the center of one of the most chilling criminal inquiries in recent memory.

# Community Members Express Disbelief and Fear

The shock that rippled through Leongatha and neighboring Korumburra was profound. These were small towns where people generally knew each other by name, where neighbors were trusted, and community ties ran deep. The deaths of three beloved residents under such bizarre and disturbing circumstances left the community reeling. Vigils were held. Flowers and handwritten notes were left outside the church where Ian Wilkinson had preached. The townspeople were not only grieving—they were bewildered.

For many, the idea that someone might have been poisoned—and not just by accident—was unfathomable. People questioned how something so deadly could have made it to the lunch table undetected. Others wondered aloud how they could ever look at a home-cooked meal the same way again.

Some residents rallied around Erin, believing she had simply made a tragic culinary mistake. Others, particularly those close to the Patterson and Wilkinson families, were more skeptical. Whispers and rumors began to circulate: Had there been tensions in the family? Could Erin have meant harm? Was there more to the story than what was being reported?

Fear quickly spread beyond the immediate families. Local mushroom foragers began receiving questions and calls from worried neighbors. Restaurants in nearby towns reported customers asking whether their mushrooms were locally sourced. The incident had planted a seed of mistrust—one that could not be easily uprooted.

# Speculation Grows Over Whether It Was Accidental or Deliberate

As the days wore on, speculation intensified. Erin's continued silence and absence from public view only fueled curiosity. In the absence of formal charges or clear answers from police, the public was left to speculate. Was it a terrible mistake—a tragic case of misidentifying wild mushrooms? Or had something more sinister taken place?

The police were careful in their public statements, emphasizing that the investigation was ongoing and that they were keeping all possibilities open. But in interviews and on social media, public opinion began to splinter. One camp believed Erin was the victim of a horrible misunderstanding—perhaps she'd picked wild mushrooms thinking they were edible, or had unknowingly purchased contaminated ingredients. The other camp was less forgiving, pointing to inconsistencies in her story, the fact that she hadn't suffered the same fate as her guests, and the mysterious disposal of a food dehydrator shortly after the lunch.

Media analysts, food safety experts, and even toxicologists were brought in by television shows and radio programs to weigh in. Some highlighted how easy it was to mistake death caps for edible mushrooms. Others questioned how someone could cook such a dish without knowing exactly what kind of ingredients they were using.

The uncertainty was agonizing for the families involved and deeply unsettling for the public. Each new detail, whether confirmed or rumored, shifted the narrative and raised new questions about Erin's intentions—and whether this was a homicide masked as a tragic accident.

# Erin Gives Initial Interviews Denying Wrongdoing

Amid mounting speculation, Erin Patterson finally broke her silence. In a written statement provided to police and later reported by the media, Erin denied any wrongdoing. She insisted that she had no reason to harm her guests and that the lunch had been cooked with the sincerest of intentions. She admitted to preparing the Beef Wellington but claimed she had used store-bought mushrooms and had eaten the meal herself, albeit a different portion than the guests.

She also addressed the now-infamous food dehydrator, which she confirmed had been discarded after lunch. According to her, it was thrown away out of panic and fear of being blamed. That admission only fueled further suspicion, with critics questioning why she would destroy potential evidence if she had nothing to hide.

Erin portrayed herself as a grieving host, someone devastated by what had happened under her roof. Yet, her statement left many questions unanswered. Why had she suffered only mild symptoms? Why had she cooked such a complex dish involving mushrooms if she wasn't sure of their safety? And if it had truly been a mistake, why hadn't she immediately come forward with the details?

Despite her denials, public doubt persisted. Her calm demeanor in interviews, her carefully worded statements, and the fact that she had not been formally charged all contributed to a growing sense of mystery—and unease. The media coverage only amplified the tension, with every public appearance, leaked detail, and police update dissected in minute detail.

# Chapter Five

## Death Cap Mushrooms — A Killer Ingredient

The silent assassin at the center of the mushroom lunch tragedy was a potent natural toxin known as amanitin, found in the death cap mushroom (Amanita phalloides). This deadly fungus is responsible for the vast majority of mushroom-related fatalities worldwide, despite being relatively rare in Australia. What makes it so dangerous is its invisibility in taste and appearance—amanitin has no noticeable smell or flavor, making it nearly impossible to detect once cooked into food.

Amanitin specifically targets the liver and kidneys, organs that are essential for filtering toxins from the blood and maintaining metabolic stability. Once ingested, the toxin begins disrupting RNA polymerase II, an enzyme critical for protein synthesis. In layman's terms, it stops cells from making the proteins they need to survive. As a result, internal organ systems begin to fail, leading to a swift and often fatal chain reaction.

In the Patterson case, the detection of amanitin in toxicology tests shifted the tragedy from an assumed foodborne illness to a suspected poisoning—accidental or intentional. The presence of such a lethal compound raised immediate red flags for investigators, especially when combined with the circumstances of the

meal and Erin Patterson's inconsistent
explanations.

## Symptoms: Delayed Onset, Organ Failure, Especially the Liver and Kidneys

One of the most deceptive aspects of death cap poisoning is the delayed onset of symptoms. After ingesting the mushroom, a person may feel completely normal for six to twelve hours. This "latency phase" often leads victims to believe they've dodged a bad meal, only for the real symptoms to erupt violently afterward.

The first stage is gastrointestinal: severe vomiting, diarrhea, cramping, and dehydration. While this stage is often mistaken for common food poisoning, it's only the beginning. A brief period of apparent recovery may follow, leading patients to believe they're improving. In reality, the toxin is silently attacking their liver and kidneys, where irreversible damage is taking place.

By the time most victims reach the hospital and undergo diagnosis, liver enzymes are spiking, and kidney function is rapidly deteriorating. Without immediate intervention—often requiring a liver transplant—the survival rate plummets. This makes early recognition of symptoms and toxin exposure critical, though it's rarely possible due to the nature of the poison.

In the Leongatha incident, the four guests experienced this exact pattern. They fell ill after the meal, seemed to worsen in sync, and within days, three were dead. The fourth, Ian Wilkinson, only survived after undergoing a liver transplant, highlighting both the severity of the toxin and the narrow window for medical intervention.

# Easily Mistaken for Edible Mushrooms

Death cap mushrooms are particularly treacherous because they look unremarkably similar to several edible varieties, especially when young. In their early growth stage, they can be easily confused with field mushrooms or paddy straw mushrooms, both commonly used in cooking. Their caps are pale greenish or yellowish with a smooth surface, and they often grow near oak and chestnut trees—trees commonly found in Australian gardens and public parks.

This visual similarity makes them a major risk to amateur foragers or untrained cooks who may harvest wild mushrooms without understanding the dangers. In Erin Patterson's case, one of the most pressing questions investigators sought to answer was: Where did the mushrooms come from? Were they wild-picked, purchased, or given by someone else?

Erin claimed in her statement that the mushrooms were a mix of store-bought button mushrooms and dried mushrooms from an Asian grocery store. However, the forensic results indicated the presence of Amanita phalloides, which does not grow in commercially farmed or imported mushroom products. This contradiction raised deep suspicion, particularly given the preparation method involving finely chopped or possibly rehydrated mushrooms, which could easily conceal their identity.

# Fatal if Not Treated Early

There is no known antidote for amanitin poisoning. Once ingested, treatment becomes a race against time. Supportive care is critical: intravenous fluids, activated charcoal (if administered early), and medications to protect the liver. In most cases of advanced poisoning, liver transplantation remains the only chance of survival.

This was evident in the Patterson case, where only Ian Wilkinson, the sole survivor, lived because he received a transplant in time. The other three guests—Don and Gail Patterson and Heather Wilkinson—were too far gone by the time aggressive treatment could begin.

Even in countries with advanced medical systems, death cap poisoning has a high mortality rate. According to toxicology data, the fatality rate ranges from 30% to 50%, depending on how quickly the patient is hospitalized and diagnosed. Unfortunately, the deceptive onset of symptoms often delays critical care, giving the toxin time to do irreversible damage.

The fact that three people died within such a short span underscored just how lethal these mushrooms are—and how out of place they seemed in a home-cooked meal.

# Uncommon in Domestic Food Poisonings, More So in Deliberate Cases

Death cap poisoning is rare in domestic settings. Most known incidents involve wild foraging gone wrong, often by tourists or newcomers unfamiliar with local flora. In Australia, occasional cases have been reported, but they are nearly always linked to mistaken identity in mushroom hunting. The notion of someone deliberately incorporating Amanita phalloides into a dish served to others is nearly unheard of.

This rarity is what made the Patterson case so shocking. If it were indeed a deliberate act, it would mark one of the few known instances where death caps were used intentionally to kill.

Poisoning with such mushrooms would require a level of knowledge—either about their lethality or about how to disguise them—that isn't common among average home cooks.

For investigators, this fact raised more red flags. How did death cap mushrooms make it into Erin's kitchen? Did she understand what they were? Was she careless or calculating? The possibility that someone might have chosen death caps as a murder weapon—one that could mimic accidental food poisoning—deepened the case's complexity and horror.

# Chapter Six

## Erin's Shifting Story

In her earliest public explanation, Erin Patterson maintained that the mushrooms she used in the Beef Wellington came from an Asian grocery store. According to her account, she had purchased a packet of dried mushrooms that she believed were safe and intended for culinary use. This statement was her attempt to explain how potentially contaminated or dangerous mushrooms had ended up in the lunch, and she was quick to deny any knowledge of their deadly potential.

By emphasizing that the mushrooms were store-bought, Erin sought to position herself as an innocent cook who had unknowingly prepared a tainted meal. This claim was meant to deflect suspicion and cast the tragedy as a freak accident—a mistake anyone could have made. However, toxicology results later showed that Amanita phalloides, or death cap mushrooms, were the likely cause of poisoning, raising immediate doubts about the credibility of her explanation. These mushrooms are not found in commercially sold dried mushroom products in Australia, especially not in reputable Asian groceries, according to food safety authorities.

# Later Added That She Also Used Dried Mushrooms from Her Pantry

As scrutiny increased and investigators probed the source of the deadly meal more deeply, Erin revised her account. She stated that, in addition to the mushrooms bought at the Asian store, she had also used some dried mushrooms from her pantry. This sudden addition introduced ambiguity and suspicion.

The idea that she had used two separate mushroom sources, without being entirely sure of their origins, weakened her earlier insistence that the ingredients were all store-bought and safe. It also added logistical complexity to the case: Where had the pantry mushrooms come from? Were they leftovers from a foraging trip?

Had someone given them to her? Could they have been stored improperly or misidentified?

These questions remained unanswered, and the shift in her narrative appeared to some as an effort to cover inconsistencies. Investigators noted the timing of the revision, which came after media outlets began highlighting the improbability of store-bought mushrooms containing deadly toxins. The change in her story did little to ease public concern and only intensified speculation that Erin was withholding the full truth.

# Stated She Never Intended to Harm Anyone

Throughout her statements, Erin repeatedly insisted that she never intended to harm anyone. She described the lunch as a heartfelt gesture—a way to reconnect with her estranged in-laws and extend peace during a difficult post-divorce period. This explanation framed her as a victim of terrible circumstances rather than a perpetrator of premeditated harm.

According to her account, the lunch was meant to bring people together, not tear them apart. Erin claimed to be devastated by the outcome and maintained that she had no motive to kill or injure anyone. She pointed out that she was still in contact with her ex-husband's family, especially Don and Gail Patterson, and that she had wanted to preserve a cordial relationship for the sake of family unity.

While her tone in interviews and statements was composed, critics argued that her emotional detachment seemed incongruous with the gravity of the situation. To some, her denial of intent came across as rehearsed or overly calculated. Investigators were especially interested in whether her denial of intent would hold up when compared with physical evidence and her evolving statements.

# Claimed to Have Been Hospitalized
# with Symptoms Herself

In an attempt to support her narrative of innocence, Erin stated that she, too, had suffered symptoms after the meal and had been hospitalized. She claimed to have experienced gastrointestinal distress similar to the other guests, though not as severe. According to Erin, this was proof that she had no idea the food was dangerous—why would she poison herself?

Hospital records confirmed that she had indeed sought medical attention after lunch. However, the degree of her symptoms was notably mild compared to the violent and ultimately fatal reactions suffered by the others. This discrepancy raised further doubts.

Toxicologists and investigators began examining whether she may have eaten a different portion of the meal or deliberately consumed only a small amount of the dish. It was also unclear whether she had taken any measures to induce vomiting or flush her system after the meal—something that might point to foreknowledge of the danger.

This part of her story walked a delicate line. On one hand, it bolstered her claim of innocence. On the other hand, it introduced the possibility that she had staged symptoms to protect herself from suspicion.

# Contradictions Noted by Police and Media

By now, Erin's narrative had changed several times. What began as a simple explanation—that she used store-bought mushrooms in good faith—evolved into a more complicated story involving multiple sources of mushrooms, vague pantry contents, and questions of symptom severity. These contradictions did not go unnoticed.

Police detectives, while cautious in public statements, acknowledged the inconsistencies in Erin's account and emphasized that they were being closely examined. The media amplified the story further, publishing side-by-side comparisons of her statements, pointing out discrepancies, and quoting experts who challenged the plausibility of her version of events.

Among the most glaring issues:

- The lack of clarity on where the pantry mushrooms came from.

- Her disposal of the food dehydrator after the incident—an action that appeared suspicious in the absence of a clear explanation.

- Her reported hospital stay didn't align with the level of poisoning others suffered.

- The sudden revisions to her account only occurred after certain facts became public.

As investigators continued their search for hard evidence, public trust in Erin Patterson's narrative began to erode. The more she spoke, the more questions arose—many of which still had no answers.

# Chapter Seven

## The Dehydrator and the Deleted Files

One of the most pivotal discoveries in the investigation was a food dehydrator linked to Erin Patterson. The appliance had been discarded at a nearby waste facility, an act that quickly drew police attention. It wasn't just the timing that raised suspicions—it was what the dehydrator represented: a possible tool used in the preparation of the fatal meal.

Authorities traced the dehydrator to Erin's residence, identifying it as one she had previously used and owned. The fact that it ended up at the tip shortly after the poisoning incident added a layer of potential intent—or at the very least, suggested an effort to eliminate something tied to the meal.

Erin later admitted she had thrown out the dehydrator but denied doing so to destroy evidence. She explained that the appliance was old and rarely used, and claimed its disposal was unrelated to the tragedy. Investigators, however, were not convinced by the timing. With three guests already deceased and the public reeling from the horror of the story, disposing of a potential kitchen instrument linked to the deadly lunch appeared deeply suspicious.

# Police Allege It Was Used to Prepare the Mushrooms

The presence of the dehydrator—and its hasty disposal—became more troubling as forensic evidence mounted. Police investigators alleged the appliance had been used to prepare the mushrooms served in the Beef Wellington. A food dehydrator, typically used to preserve fruits, vegetables, or herbs, could also be used to dry mushrooms—intentionally or inadvertently concentrating any toxins they contain.

Drying mushrooms doesn't neutralize their chemical compounds;, in the case of death cap mushrooms, it may intensify the potency of the toxin by removing water content. If toxic mushrooms were indeed dehydrated, the result would be more lethal per gram when added to food.

Police believed that the dehydrator could hold residue, spores, or traces of the deadly Amanita phalloides. Unfortunately, by the time they retrieved it, the appliance had already been contaminated or compromised by exposure at the waste site. Still, the simple fact that Erin disposed of it after serving the meal became a critical detail in building a timeline of actions and intent.

# Erin's Phone Was Factory Reset

The investigation took another dramatic turn when police examined Erin Patterson's mobile phone. According to reports, the device had been factory reset, effectively wiping its contents. This action removed call logs, messages, photos, browsing history, and other potentially valuable digital data.

A factory reset is an uncommon step for an average user, especially during the unfolding of a high-profile death investigation. Erin's decision to reset the phone came after lunch but before her formal police interviews, which raised alarm bells for investigators. They questioned whether the reset was a routine act or a calculated effort to remove incriminating evidence.

Digital forensic experts were called in to try and retrieve any residual data from backups or cloud storage. Although some information was recoverable, large chunks of the device's history were lost permanently due to the reset. This gap in evidence became a significant challenge in tracing Erin's digital activity before and after the fatal lunch.

## Several Digital Files Deleted, Raising Questions About Intent

In addition to the reset phone, investigators discovered that several files and communications had been deleted from Erin's other devices and online accounts. These included emails, browser records, and messaging data, some of which were believed to be related to recipe searches and potential communications with others regarding the meal.

The nature and timing of the deletions fueled growing suspicion that Erin may have attempted to cover her digital tracks. Investigators began to examine whether she had looked up topics such as "toxic mushrooms," "death cap identification," or "symptoms of mushroom poisoning." While no single search proved guilt, the pattern of deletion pointed to deliberate curation of her digital footprint.

Forensic teams cross-referenced known deletions with data recovered from cloud backups, router logs, and other synced devices. Though some files were successfully retrieved, many were beyond recovery. The selective nature of the data deletion—as opposed to broad or accidental erasure—added to the perception that she had something to hide.

# Investigators Retrieved Internet Search History and Deleted Texts

Despite the loss of data from Erin's primary device, investigators managed to recover fragments of internet search history and deleted text messages through secondary sources. This included information backed up to cloud servers, metadata from synced applications, and data pulled from third-party communications apps.

Some of the recovered search terms were consistent with someone researching mushroom recipes. However, some queries suggested an awareness of mushroom toxicity, and even references to how to treat food poisoning and organ failure symptoms, searches conducted around the same time as the poisoning.

In addition, texts between Erin and other individuals—including her children and former in-laws—were partially restored. While many of the messages were benign, there were a few that investigators considered "of interest" due to their timing or tone. These texts were not immediately made public, but their contents reportedly informed the broader direction of the inquiry.

The digital evidence, combined with the physical discovery of the dehydrator, formed the backbone of the prosecution's suspicions. While circumstantial on its own, it painted a picture of someone who may have tried to erase traces of a lethal act, whether accidental or deliberate.

# Chapter Eight

## A Pattern of Deceit

In the wake of the mushroom lunch deaths, scrutiny intensified not only on the circumstances of the fatal meal but also on Erin Patterson's past behavior. One particularly troubling detail surfaced from her personal history: she had allegedly falsely claimed to have cancer in an earlier period of her life.

According to those close to Erin, she once told people that she was undergoing cancer treatment. It was later discovered that no such diagnosis had ever been confirmed, and no medical records substantiated her claim. Those who had offered her emotional and sometimes financial support during that time felt misled, describing the revelation as deeply unsettling.

This incident wasn't simply a strange or isolated lie—it pointed to what investigators began to consider a potential pattern of manipulative behavior. Police and behavioral experts reviewing Erin's background began to evaluate whether the false cancer claim had been an early instance of deception designed to evoke sympathy and control how others perceived her. If Erin was capable of fabricating a life-threatening illness to gain support, it raised questions about the sincerity of her recent public statements regarding the poisoning deaths.

While not directly linked to the mushroom lunch, the cancer claim came to be viewed as a precedent of emotional manipulation—a troubling sign that Erin was capable of using falsehoods for personal advantage.

## Erin's Ex-Husband, Simon Patterson, Had a History of Unexplained Illness

Adding to the web of suspicion was the medical history of Erin's ex-husband, Simon Patterson, who had suffered a serious and unexplained illness in 2022, just a year before the fatal lunch. Simon, a respected local educator and sportsman, had been hospitalized for an extended period due to what was initially described as a mystery gastrointestinal illness.

At the time, his condition had deteriorated so rapidly that doctors feared for his life. Simon reportedly spent weeks in intensive care, experiencing multiple organ failure, and narrowly survived. The cause of his illness was never publicly confirmed. Though some believed it could have been a rare infection or autoimmune response, others—especially after the lunch incident—began to look back on his case with new suspicion.

As the details of the mushroom poisoning emerged, investigators revisited Simon's medical files and timeline. The fact that he had suffered a life-threatening but undiagnosed illness while still connected to Erin Patterson raised uncomfortable questions. Could his mysterious episode have also involved something ingested? Could it have been another case of mushroom poisoning—or something similar?

No official charges or accusations were made concerning Simon's illness, but it became a crucial thread in the broader narrative surrounding Erin. If she had any role in his past health crisis, it could point to premeditated behavior or a deeper pattern of harmful conduct.

# Simon Was Invited to the Lunch But Did Not Attend

Perhaps the most chilling detail in the case was that Simon Patterson had been invited to the lunch on July 29, 2023—the same meal that left three of his family members dead and one hospitalized in critical condition. According to both Erin and police sources, Simon had been on the guest list for the now-infamous gathering. He ultimately declined the invitation and did not attend.

His absence proved fateful. Had he been there, Simon may have consumed the same meal and met the same tragic end. The coincidence was not lost on police, who regarded it as potentially significant in assessing Erin's intentions. If the meal had been deliberately poisoned, then knowing Simon had been invited raised serious questions: Was he a target? Did Erin know or anticipate that he wouldn't attend? Or was his absence a lucky escape?

The invitation was initially cited by Erin as a gesture of goodwill, part of an effort to mend fractured family relationships. But some investigators saw it as a calculated move—perhaps an effort to deflect suspicion by including Simon in the gathering or, more darkly, as part of a plan that had not fully unfolded.

To Simon, the close call was harrowing. He has remained largely silent in public, but those close to him have said he now views that missed lunch as a turning point in his life. Whether it was intuition, circumstance, or sheer luck that kept him away, his nonattendance became a powerful detail in the unraveling of the case.

# Police Viewed Her Behavior as Strategic and Misleading

Across interviews, witness statements, and public communications, law enforcement officers began to form a consistent picture of Erin Patterson's conduct in the aftermath of the tragedy. Police described her behavior as strategic, evasive, and at times overtly misleading.

From the shifting stories about where the mushrooms came from, to the discarding of the food dehydrator, and the factory-resetting of her phone, authorities saw a pattern. Even Erin's emotional demeanor raised eyebrows; though she expressed sorrow, many noted a lack of consistent affect or urgency in her public appearances.

Detectives emphasized that Erin's cooperative moments were often paired with contradictory actions, such as refusing to provide key documents without legal pressure or omitting critical details until they surfaced through external sources. The inconsistencies were not merely frustrating for the investigation—they were potentially incriminating.

To those leading the case, Erin Patterson came across not as an overwhelmed woman blindsided by tragedy, but as someone calculating her every step, adjusting her narrative with each new development in the media or forensic results. That perception fed into the decision to ultimately treat her not as a bystander or an unlucky cook, but as the central suspect in what they believed to be Australia's most bizarre and deliberate triple homicide.

# Chapter Nine

## Arrest and Charges

On the morning of November 2, 2023, Erin Patterson was formally arrested by detectives from Victoria Police's Homicide Squad. The arrest occurred at her home in Leongatha, where officers arrived with a search warrant and took her into custody without incident. After months of speculation, media scrutiny, and investigative work, the case had reached a critical turning point.

The arrest was the result of what police described as a "methodical and detailed" investigation that had involved forensic testing, digital data recovery, interviews with dozens of witnesses, and toxicology reports. Erin had remained a person of interest throughout the case, but until that day, no formal charges had been laid.

The arrest triggered a wave of national and international media coverage. Camera crews gathered outside police stations, and journalists revisited every detail of the fatal lunch that had shocked the country just a few months earlier. The arrest confirmed what many had suspected: that authorities believed the poisonings were not accidental.

Following her arrest, Erin Patterson was charged with three counts of murder. These charges related directly to the deaths of:

- Gail Patterson, her former mother-in-law

- Don Patterson, her former father-in-law

- Heather Wilkinson, Gail's sister

The victims had all died within days of eating the Beef Wellington Erin had prepared. Autopsies and toxicology reports confirmed the presence of amatoxins, the deadly compounds found in death cap mushrooms. Based on the evidence collected—including witness statements, forensic traces, and circumstantial factors like the disposal of the dehydrator—police determined there was sufficient basis to pursue murder charges.

Each count of murder carried a potential life sentence under Australian law, and the charges were considered among the most serious ever laid in a regional Victorian criminal case in recent history.

In addition to the murder charges, Erin was also charged with one count of attempted murder. This charge was concerning Ian Wilkinson, the husband of Heather Wilkinson and a local Baptist pastor.

Ian had survived the meal but only after being hospitalized for weeks in intensive care. He had undergone multiple organ support treatments and spent significant time in recovery. According to police, his survival was not due to any lack of intent on the part of the accused but rather the result of immediate and extensive medical intervention.

The attempted murder charge indicated that investigators believed Erin had served all four guests a poisoned meal knowingly, with no distinction made between those who died and the one who narrowly survived.

# Bail Was Denied Initially

Following her arraignment, Erin Patterson appeared in court where she applied for bail. Prosecutors strongly opposed the request, arguing that she posed both a flight risk and a potential risk to public safety. They also emphasized concerns that she may interfere with witnesses or tamper with remaining evidence if released.

The judge sided with the prosecution and denied bail, citing the severity of the charges and the substantial evidence already gathered by investigators. Erin was remanded in custody at a women's correctional facility, where she would await further court proceedings.

The decision to keep her in custody was a reflection not only of the gravity of the alleged crimes but also of the extraordinary public interest surrounding the case. Supporters of the victims expressed relief, while legal commentators noted that the denial of bail was consistent with murder cases of this magnitude.

# Case Formally Enters Pre-Trial Proceedings

With the charges officially laid and bail denied, the case entered the pre-trial phase. During this stage, prosecutors were required to present evidence sufficient to justify a full criminal trial. This included submitting toxicology results, forensic analysis, digital records, and witness testimony.

The court also heard from the defense team, which began to outline its strategy, suggesting that the poisonings had been a tragic accident, not a calculated crime. Erin maintained her not-guilty plea on all charges.

The pre-trial process involved committal hearings, where a magistrate reviewed the evidence to determine whether there was a prima facie case to answer in a higher court. These hearings were closely watched by the media and the public, with every appearance scrutinized for signs of new revelations or shifting legal arguments.

While a trial date had not yet been set, the formal beginning of legal proceedings ensured that the case would soon move from the realm of police investigation into the arena of criminal justice—a long-awaited next chapter in one of Australia's most unsettling murder cases in recent memory.

# Chapter Ten

## The Mushroom Murders Trial Begins

After months of mounting anticipation and legal maneuvering, the trial of Erin Patterson began in April 2025 at the Supreme Court of Victoria. Security at the courthouse was tight, with uniformed officers stationed around the premises and a heavy media presence assembled outside. Dozens of journalists, reporters, and camera crews gathered each day to cover what had been described as one of the most bizarre and shocking homicide trials in Australian legal history.

The courtroom was packed with observers: family members of the victims, members of the public, legal analysts, and international correspondents. Inside, the atmosphere was tense and charged with emotion. As Erin Patterson entered the courtroom for the first day of proceedings, all eyes were on her. Dressed plainly and flanked by her legal team, she sat silently as the charges against her were read aloud again—three counts of murder, one count of attempted murder.

The trial was scheduled to span several weeks, allowing time for forensic evidence, witness testimony, and legal arguments to be examined in full.

# Prosecution Argued Erin Acted Knowingly and Deliberately

The prosecution opened their case with a stark message to the jury: Erin Patterson had intentionally served a fatal meal to her former in-laws and their guests, knowing the mushrooms she used were deadly death caps.

The Crown's lead prosecutor laid out the theory that Erin had deliberately laced the Beef Wellington with toxic mushrooms to eliminate her former in-laws and potentially her ex-husband, Simon Patterson, who had originally been invited to the lunch. Prosecutors emphasized several key details they argued supported intent:

- Erin had previously researched toxic mushrooms online.

- She discarded a food dehydrator believed to have been used in preparing the meal—an act the prosecution framed as an attempt to destroy evidence.

- She provided shifting explanations about where the mushrooms came from and why she was not sickened.

- She invited Simon Patterson, who ultimately didn't attend, suggesting a broader plan.

Expert witnesses testified about the lethal nature of death cap mushrooms, explaining that even small amounts could kill and that they were easily distinguishable from edible varieties. Forensic analysts presented evidence of amatoxins in the victims' autopsy reports, and pathologists explained the symptoms that had led to the deaths.

The prosecution argued that Erin's actions reflected premeditation and manipulation. They reminded the jury of her alleged past falsehoods, including a previous claim of having cancer, and they urged the court to consider whether this case fit a larger pattern of deceit and control.

# Defense Claimed It Was a Tragic Accident

Erin Patterson's legal team presented a very different picture. According to the defense, the deaths were not the result of murder, but rather the outcome of a tragic accident born from ignorance.

Her lawyers maintained that Erin did not know that the mushrooms she used were dangerous. They suggested she had purchased them from a local Asian grocery store, believing them to be ordinary dried mushrooms commonly used in home cooking. The defense asserted that she had no motive to harm her former in-laws and had invited them to lunch as a sincere gesture of reconciliation.

The defense team dismissed the claims of premeditation, framing them as speculation and circumstantial. Regarding the food dehydrator, they argued Erin had thrown it away because it was old and broken, not to hide evidence. As for the lack of illness on her part, they pointed out that Erin had been briefly hospitalized, though not as severely as her guests—a sign that she had consumed at least part of the same meal.

Her lawyers emphasized that accidental poisonings from wild mushrooms, while rare, do happen—and that this case had been blown out of proportion by public hysteria and media bias. They portrayed Erin as a grieving and overwhelmed woman, caught in a nightmare she could neither explain nor escape.

Witnesses for the defense included character references who described Erin as nonviolent and family-oriented, and experts who testified about how easily misidentified wild mushrooms can be, particularly when dried or processed.

The defense closed by asking the jury to consider the possibility of human error, rather than malicious intent, reminding them of the burden of proof the prosecution carried.

# Case Drew International Media Attention

From the very first day of the trial, the case attracted massive international interest. Headlines about the "Mushroom Murders" appeared not just across Australia but in the United Kingdom, the United States, Canada, and Asia. True crime forums exploded with speculation, and major networks ran daily updates on the proceedings.

Much of the fascination stemmed from the case's unusual nature—a seemingly ordinary family lunch in a quiet Australian town turning into a deadly tragedy involving foraged mushrooms. The ingredients were dramatic and deeply unsettling: a home-cooked meal, the quiet mother at its center, and three bodies in its aftermath.

The media coverage also amplified public opinion, which was deeply divided. Some saw Erin Patterson as a cold-blooded killer hiding behind a suburban facade. Others saw a woman whose life had been upended by coincidence and misfortune.

The courtroom was regularly surrounded by camera crews, and each legal development was scrutinized on morning shows, evening news, and in online columns. Legal experts weighed in daily, and the trial came to represent a cultural fascination with domestic crime, food safety, and the hidden dynamics of family estrangement.

As the testimony continued and the jury listened to days of often harrowing evidence, one thing became clear: the outcome of the case would leave a lasting imprint on Australian legal history, regardless of the verdict.

# Chapter Eleven

## Eight Days on the Stand

Erin Patterson took the witness stand in her defense—a move both anticipated and controversial. What followed was a grueling stretch of eight consecutive days of testimony, during which she answered questions from both her defense team and the Crown prosecutors. Her decision to testify was a high-stakes gamble, one that placed her in full view of the jury and the public, with every word and gesture recorded, analyzed, and interpreted.

Throughout the eight days, Erin faced long hours of questioning. She sat for hours at a time under courtroom lighting, often with the media gallery filled. Her voice was steady at times, wavering at others, and her facial expressions ranged from solemn to visibly distressed. It was one of the longest testimonies by a defendant in recent Australian criminal court history—a fact that underscored the complexity and intensity of the case.

## Maintained: She Never Intended Harm

From the outset, Erin was adamant: she had never meant to harm anyone. She testified that she had prepared the Beef Wellington as a "peace offering," hoping to rebuild strained ties with her former in-laws. She insisted that the mushrooms she used had been purchased from an Asian grocery store, and she had no idea they were toxic.

"I loved them," she said tearfully when asked about Gail and Don Patterson. "I never would have done anything to hurt them."

Her testimony painted a picture of a woman overwhelmed by grief and confusion after the tragedy. She described her emotional collapse after learning the guests had become ill, and how she had cooperated with police interviews despite growing suspicions against her. She admitted to throwing out the food dehydrator, but insisted it was a coincidence, not an attempt to hide evidence.

Throughout her testimony, she returned repeatedly to the central claim of her defense: it was a tragic accident, not a deliberate act.

# Struggled Under Prosecutorial Cross-Examination

While Erin's defense testimony was composed and emotional, her time under cross-examination was markedly more difficult. The Crown prosecutor pressed her relentlessly, challenging her statements and raising inconsistencies from previous interviews.

At times, Erin appeared visibly rattled. She hesitated when asked about the timeline of her shopping trip, the origin of the mushrooms, and her decision to discard the dehydrator. The prosecution played audio recordings of her earlier police interviews, pointing out where her explanations had shifted over time.

They questioned why she had survived the meal while her guests had perished, and why she had initially told investigators that her children had been at the lunch, only to later recant. They asked why Simon Patterson, her ex-husband, had declined to attend—and whether she had anticipated his absence.

As the questions intensified, Erin's calm began to fray. She wept openly on the stand, prompting her defense to request breaks. The prosecutor, unmoved, returned again and again to one central argument: Erin's story didn't add up.

Observers noted that she often gave vague responses or said she "couldn't remember" key details. The Crown used this to suggest that she was deliberately evasive—a strategy meant to avoid acknowledging her alleged guilt.

# Her Demeanor and Tone Became Part of Public Debate

Outside the courtroom, public interest in Erin's testimony was fervent. Daily news bulletins analyzed her body language, vocal tone, and emotional outbursts. Was she genuine or performing? Was her sorrow real, or was it a tactic designed to influence the jury?

Talk shows dissected her courtroom demeanor. Some commentators described her as a woman under unbearable pressure, crumbling as she relived a traumatic event. Others saw strategic vulnerability, meant to humanize her before the jury and cast doubt on the prosecution's narrative.

Social media platforms buzzed with commentary—some sympathetic, others scathing. Viewers debated whether her testimony revealed guilt, innocence, or something far more complex. Hashtags like #MushroomTrial, #ErinPatterson, and #PoisonedLunch trended nationally, with every clip and quote sparking waves of opinion.

Legal experts weighed in as well, noting that a defendant's testimony can often be a turning point, especially in cases driven more by circumstantial evidence than direct proof.

By the time Erin stepped down from the witness box after eight emotionally charged days, the public had seen a full portrait of the accused: a grieving woman, a possible manipulator, a victim of bad luck, or a calculating killer. It would now be up to the jury to decide which version they believed.

# Chapter Twelve

## Survivor on the Stand — Ian Wilkinson

When Ian Wilkinson took the stand, the courtroom fell silent. His appearance was frail, a stark contrast to the robust local pastor once well known in the Korumburra community. Now, he was not just the grieving husband of a victim, but the sole survivor of the fatal lunch. His presence was both a symbol of resilience and a living witness to the horror that unfolded on that fateful day.

Wilkinson recounted, in calm and deliberate detail, the immediate aftermath of the lunch. Within hours of returning home, he began feeling unwell. Symptoms rapidly escalated—nausea, stomach cramps, vomiting.

What started as what seemed to be mild food poisoning soon turned into something far more severe. By the next day, he was rushed to the hospital and admitted to the intensive care unit.

Medical records presented during the trial confirmed that Wilkinson had suffered multiple organ failures, including his kidneys, liver, and gastrointestinal tract. His condition deteriorated so quickly that physicians described his survival as "borderline miraculous." He was placed in a medically induced coma as doctors fought to stabilize him, uncertain if he would make it through the night.

# Underwent a Liver Transplant

Wilkinson's condition continued to worsen despite aggressive treatment. Blood tests showed dangerously high levels of amatoxins—the deadly compound found in Amanita phalloides, commonly known as death cap mushrooms. The damage to his liver was irreversible.

A liver transplant became his only chance at survival.

The court heard from the medical staff involved in the procedure. They confirmed that Wilkinson was airlifted to a specialist transplant unit and placed at the top of the urgent recipient list. The transplant was performed within days of the poisoning, a delicate and high-risk operation that ultimately saved his life.

Wilkinson testified that although he had no memory of the surgery itself, he woke up weeks later in recovery, devastated to learn that his wife, Heather Wilkinson, had not survived—nor had Don and Gail Patterson.

The transplant left him physically weakened, with a lifetime dependency on anti-rejection medication, dietary restrictions, and compromised immunity. Yet it also gave him the rare chance to speak for the others who could not.

# Described Shock and Grief Over Losing His Wife

Wilkinson's voice trembled when he spoke about Heather. Married for decades, the couple had built a life centered around faith, community, and family. Her loss, he said, was not just personal—it was the collapse of a shared existence.

He recalled the moment he was told she had died while he lay in recovery. The impact was so crushing that he could not bring himself to speak for days. "I survived, but everything I knew was gone," he told the court.

Wilkinson expressed grief, confusion, and lingering disbelief, struggling to reconcile the tragedy with the casual lunch they had attended at Erin Patterson's home. "We went in friendship. We left in silence."

He also spoke of the ripple effects the tragedy had on his church and local community. People who once gathered for worship were now gathering in mourning. He had not returned to the pulpit, and said that public life—once his calling—had become deeply painful.

Despite his visible sorrow, Wilkinson maintained a composed and dignified presence throughout his testimony, earning quiet respect from both legal teams and courtroom observers alike.

# His Survival Allowed Prosecutors to Reconstruct the Timeline

As the only surviving guest from the fatal lunch, Ian Wilkinson's testimony was vital to the prosecution's case. His account helped establish the exact timeline of the poisoning, clarifying how quickly symptoms began, how they progressed, and when emergency services were called.

Prosecutors used his statements to reconstruct the hours following the meal, comparing his physical reactions with those of the other victims. His timeline matched what forensic toxicologists later confirmed: that symptoms of amatoxin poisoning typically appear 6 to 12 hours after ingestion, followed by liver and kidney failure if left untreated.

Wilkinson's statement that the food "tasted perfectly normal" supported expert claims that death caps can be nearly impossible to detect by flavor alone—a detail that further undermined the defense's argument that Erin Patterson was unaware of their danger.

Most importantly, Wilkinson confirmed that Erin herself had not appeared sick during or after the meal. She had not expressed concerns about the ingredients. She had not called to check on the guests until well after symptoms had developed.

For prosecutors, Wilkinson was more than a sympathetic witness. He was the linchpin in establishing causality and intent—a voice that transformed an otherwise silent event into a timeline that made logical and legal sense.

# Chapter Thirteen

## The Verdict

After months of courtroom drama, extensive witness testimony, and relentless media coverage, the highly anticipated verdict in Erin Patterson's case was finally delivered on July 7, 2025. The courtroom was packed—legal teams, reporters, relatives of the victims, and members of the public all waited in heavy silence as the jury foreperson stood to announce the outcome.

The deliberations had lasted several days, reflecting the complex nature of the evidence presented. Jurors had to weigh emotional testimony, circumstantial links, forensic reports, and Erin's own words from the stand. As the clock struck midday, the judge asked the jury if they had reached a unanimous decision. The answer was yes.

The moment was charged with tension, and the atmosphere was nearly unbreathable.

# Erin Patterson Found Guilty on All Charges

Erin Patterson was found guilty on all counts—three charges of murder and one charge of attempted murder. The courtroom erupted in a mix of gasps, tears, and whispered exchanges. Erin, seated in the dock, reportedly closed her eyes and exhaled slowly, her expression unreadable.

The judge thanked the jury for their service and emphasized the gravity of their decision. A formal sentencing hearing was scheduled for the following month, but the conviction alone marked the end of a long, grueling process that had captivated the nation.

Throughout the trial, the prosecution had argued that Erin knowingly served death cap mushrooms to her in-laws and their guests, and that her actions were deliberate and premeditated. The defense maintained her innocence, claiming it was a tragic accident. The jury, however, sided with the Crown.

For the families of Don and Gail Patterson and Heather Wilkinson, the verdict offered a sense of finality—even if it could never truly bring closure.

## Public Reaction Was Intense—Many Expressed Relief, Others Shock

The response across Australia was immediate and impassioned. Social media platforms lit up with reactions ranging from outrage to vindication. Hashtags like #MushroomVerdict and #ErinPattersonGuilty trended nationwide within minutes.

For many, the verdict was a relief—a validation of their belief that the deaths had not been accidental. Supporters of the victims' families said justice had been served and praised the jury for their careful deliberation.

Others, however, were stunned. There remained a small but vocal contingent who believed Erin's version of events—that the mushrooms had been purchased unknowingly and that she had never intended harm. Some argued that the lack of direct evidence—such as video footage, eyewitnesses, or a confession—should have resulted in reasonable doubt.

Legal experts appeared on television and in online forums to debate the implications. Some praised the thoroughness of the trial and the strength of the forensic timeline. Others cautioned that the conviction raised troubling questions about how guilt is assessed in complex, circumstantial cases.

# Media Outlets Dubbed It One of Australia's Most Bizarre Homicides

The media's treatment of the case had been intense from the beginning, but the guilty verdict sent coverage into overdrive. Major newspapers and TV networks declared it "one of the most bizarre and chilling homicide cases in Australian history."

Headlines described Erin Patterson as the "Mushroom Widow," "The Hostess Killer," and "Australia's Most Unlikely Murderer." Longform retrospectives were published overnight, recapping every twist—from the initial lunch to Erin's emotional testimony and final conviction.

Commentators marveled at the surreal elements of the case: a home-cooked meal gone deadly, the use of a naturally occurring but lethal ingredient, the absence of a traditional weapon, and the alleged killer being a quiet woman from the suburbs with no criminal history.

Documentary producers immediately began preparing in-depth specials. Streaming services reportedly scrambled for rights to dramatize the story. In the eyes of many, the Erin Patterson case had taken on a mythic quality—part cautionary tale, part true-crime legend.

And yet, beneath the sensationalism was the enduring truth: three lives were lost, one survivor was left scarred forever, and a woman now stood convicted of orchestrating a quiet, horrifying triple homicide with a plate of food.

# Chapter Fourteen

## Sentencing and the Road Ahead

With the guilty verdict delivered on July 7, 2025, the case entered its final judicial stage: sentencing. The judge announced that the sentencing phase would be scheduled for late August or early September, allowing time for victim impact statements, pre-sentencing reports, and additional legal submissions from both the prosecution and defense.

This phase would not only determine the length and conditions of Erin Patterson's imprisonment but would also serve as a platform for the families of the deceased to express their grief, anger, and hopes for justice. Australian courts typically allow such statements to be read aloud in court, giving survivors and relatives a powerful opportunity to speak directly to both the offender and the public.

Anticipation surrounding the sentencing remained high, with legal experts predicting an emotionally charged hearing likely to draw as much attention as the verdict itself.

# Erin Faces Life Imprisonment

Under Victorian law, a conviction for multiple counts of murder carries the potential for life imprisonment without parole. In Erin's case, the gravity of the crimes—three deaths and one attempted murder—placed her firmly in the highest tier of sentencing severity.

The prosecution signaled that it would argue for the maximum penalty, citing premeditation, the breach of familial trust, and the public danger posed by her actions. Prosecutors were expected to frame the incident not as a momentary lapse or error in judgment, but as a calculated act with deadly intent, carried out in the most intimate of settings: a family lunch.

Defense counsel, meanwhile, would likely seek a parole-eligible sentence, arguing that Erin had no prior criminal history, continued to claim innocence, and had already endured immense public condemnation.

Regardless of the final length imposed, Erin Patterson would almost certainly spend decades behind bars. The question was whether those years would be finite, or whether she would die in prison.

# Families of the Victims Seek Closure and Justice

For the families of Don and Gail Patterson, Heather Wilkinson, and the lone survivor Ian Wilkinson, the sentencing marked the culmination of an ordeal that began not in a courtroom, but in a suburban kitchen.

Public statements released through legal representatives and family spokespeople expressed a mix of relief and sorrow. Some described the trial as retraumatizing—forcing them to relive painful moments through testimony, photos, and forensic evidence. Others welcomed the guilty verdict as the first real step toward closure.

Still, justice—no matter how firmly delivered—could not bring back the victims. Ian Wilkinson, who had spent months recovering from multiple organ failure and the loss of his wife, was expected to deliver a personal statement at sentencing. Friends described him as "focused on honoring Heather's memory, not vengeance."

The families emphasized the importance of public understanding, hoping that the case would raise awareness not only about the lethality of death cap mushrooms but also about the hidden complexities of domestic relationships and the capacity for violence in unexpected places.

# Appeals Process Remains Open but Uncertain

Although convicted, Erin Patterson retained the right to appeal the verdict, a process that could begin within weeks after sentencing. Legal analysts noted that while appeals in high-profile murder cases are not uncommon, they are rarely successful, particularly when supported by extensive circumstantial and forensic evidence.

To succeed, Erin's legal team would need to identify procedural errors, judicial misdirection, or new exculpatory evidence that had not been available during the original trial. So far, no such grounds had been made public.

Nevertheless, given the media attention and the severity of the sentence likely to be imposed, it was anticipated that her lawyers might pursue at least an initial appeal, if only to preserve her long-term legal options.

Until then, Erin Patterson would remain in custody, likely at a high-security women's facility in Victoria, awaiting her formal sentencing while legal strategies continued behind the scenes.

## Case Raises Broader Questions About Culpability and Domestic Trust

Beyond the legalities, the Patterson mushroom case had provoked a national conversation about how Australians understand trust, intent, and danger in everyday life.

Here was a woman, with no known history of violence, accused—and now convicted—of using a homemade meal as a murder weapon. The idea that a family lunch could become a site of calculated homicide unsettled people across the country. It exposed the fragile assumptions many hold about domestic safety and the boundaries of normalcy.

Legal scholars began using the case as a teaching example, exploring how circumstantial evidence can carry weight in the absence of direct proof, and how the line between carelessness and criminal intent can blur in the public eye.

Some advocates called for clearer public warnings about toxic wild mushrooms, noting that death caps closely resemble edible varieties and can be found in populated areas. Others discussed the psychological profiles of seemingly ordinary individuals who commit extraordinary crimes.

Ultimately, the case reminded Australians that danger does not always come wearing a mask or carrying a weapon. Sometimes, it comes in a familiar kitchen, on a plate passed with a smile—and the consequences, as seen in the deaths of Don, Gail, and Heather, are both devastating and irreversible.

# Epilogue

Erin Patterson had no record of violence, no whispered history of cruelty, no past that foretold the horror that would one day unfold in her Leongatha kitchen. Her victims were not enemies or strangers—they were family. People she had once laughed with, shared holidays with, and invited into her home.

The method of murder was chilling in its mundanity: a home-cooked meal, a gesture wrapped in tradition and warmth. Yet beneath the golden crust of the Beef Wellington lay something lethal—death cap mushrooms, toxic enough to kill with only a bite. What followed was not just a tragedy, but a puzzle. Three people lost their lives. One barely survived. And the woman at the center of it all claimed it had been an accident.

Despite a trial that stretched for months, despite witness testimony, forensic reports, and a guilty verdict, the motive remained elusive. Why would a woman—reserved, intelligent, outwardly calm—plan such an intimate and deadly act? Was it rage, revenge, desperation, or something darker still?

In the end, Erin Patterson's silence spoke louder than her words. And as the doors of the courtroom closed for the last time, Australia was left with a haunting truth: some murders come not with screams or gunshots, but with quiet intention—served warm on a plate, between people who once called each other family.

Printed in Dunstable, United Kingdom